BIG BOOK OF BEGINNER'S PIANO CLASSICS

83 Favorite Pieces in Easy Piano Arrangements

BERGERAC
and
DAVID DUTKANICZ

DOVER PUBLICATIONS, INC.
Mineola, New York

Bibliographical Note

Big Book of Beginner's Piano Classics is a new compilation of works originally published by Dover Publications, Inc., in *A First Book of Classical Music* (2000), *A First Book of Chopin* (2003), and *A First Book of Great Composers* (2004), all by Bergerac, and *A First Book of Mozart* (2005), *A First Book of Beethoven* (2006), *A First Book of Bach* (2007), and *A First Book of Tchaikovsky* (2008) all by David Dutkanicz.

International Standard Book Number

ISBN-13: 978-0-486-46615-6
ISBN-10: 0-486-46615-9

Manufactured in the United States by LSC Communications
46615921   2020
www.doverpublications.com

CONTENTS

Works are arranged in alphabetical order by composer.
However, some works have been placed in such a way that it is easier to facilitate page turns.

Note

Designed especially for beginning pianists, *Big Book of Beginner's Piano Classics* will bring the joy of classical music to students of all ages. These carefully selected pieces have been arranged and simplified in order to develop the hands and ears of the performer, allowing them to experience music that otherwise would have been too difficult. Most of the works focus on a special skill: e.g., playing in octaves in the opening of Bach's *Tocatta and Fugue in D Minor*, four-part chorale playing in Tchaikovsky's *1812 Overture*, or playing with accented notes in Mussorgsky's *Hopak*. Fingerings have been provided as a suggestion, but should not be considered absolute, since each pair of hands playing these arrangements is unique. Also, phrasing and pedaling have been left open in order to make the music less daunting. These can be filled in as the student progresses.

Italian Words in the Music

adagio, very slow

adagio cantabile, very slow and songful

adagio un poco mosso, very slow with a little momentum

allegretto, moving along, but not too fast

allegretto tranquillo, moving along, but not fast, in a tranquil manner

allegro con brio, lively, with a lot of vigor

allegro molto, very fast

allegro passionate, fast and impassioned

andante, walking tempo

andante cantabile, walking tempo, in a songful manner

andante grazioso, walking tempo, in a graceful manner

andantino, a bit faster than a walking tempo

a tempo, return to the original speed

cantabile, songful

cantado, singing out

coda, a concluding section

cresc(endo), getting louder

cresc(endo) poco a poco, getting louder, little by little

dim. E rit. (diminuendo e ritardando) poca a poca, gradually quieter and slower

D. C. al Fine (da capo al Fine), return to the beginning, then go to the "Fine" (end)

dolce, gently, sweetly

espressivo, espr., expressive

Fine, end

f (forte), loud

ff (fortissimo), very loud

fz (forzando), strongly accented

ffz (molto forzando), very strongly accented

grazioso, graceful

largo, very slow, solemn

legato, smooth, connected

leggiero, lightly

lento, very slow (a bit faster than *largo*)

lento espressivo, slow and expressive

lento placido, slow and placid

L.H., left hand

maestoso, majestic, stately

marc(ato), marked, accented

mf (mezzo-forte), medium loud

moderato, at a moderate speed

moderato cantabile, songful, at a moderate speed

molto legato, very smooth and connected

molto marcato, very accented

molto rall(entando), held back a great deal

molto rit(ardando), slow down a great deal

molto staccato, very short and detached

mp (mezzo-piano), medium soft

p (piano), soft

pp (pianissimo), very soft

ppp (pianississimo), very very soft

poco a poco, little by little

poco cresc. E. rall(entando), slightly getting louder and held back

poco rall(entando), slightly held back

poco rit(ardando), slowing down a little

rall(entando), held back

rall(entando), poco a poco, held back little by little

rall(entando), E dim. poco a poco, held back and getting quieter little by little

R.H., right hand

ritardando, slowing down

sempre sostenuto, always sustained

sfz (sforzando), strongly accented

sostenuto, sost., sustained

tempo di valse, a waltz

tranquillo, tranquil

vivace, very fast, lively

Johann Sebastian Bach

(Germany, 1685–1750)

Minuet

Bach's young wife, Anna Magdalena, brought great happiness to his household. Together they kept little notebooks that were full of the most miscellaneous matters, including the manuscript of this graceful minuet that he composed for her in 1722, when he was 37 years old. Such court dances were extremely popular among the nobility of Europe.

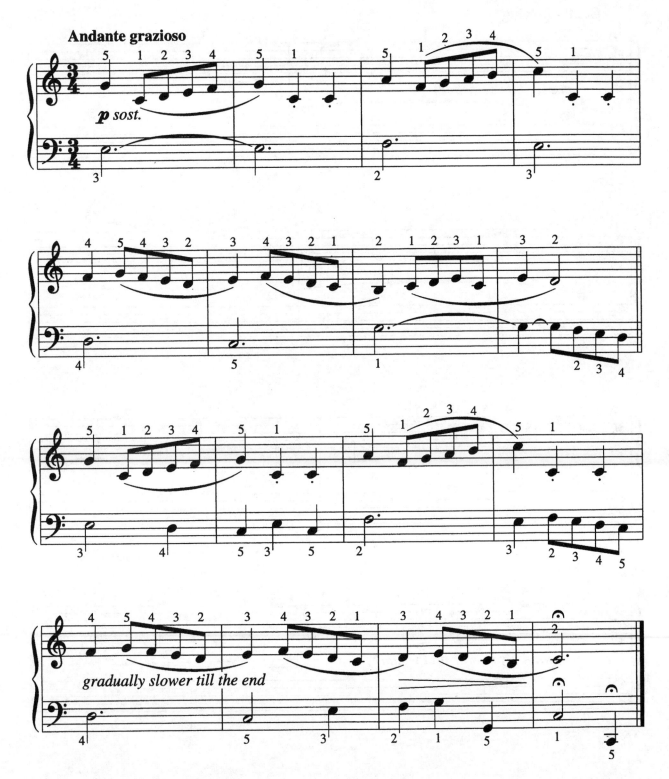

(Germany, 1685–1750)

SHEEP MAY SAFELY GRAZE

Five years before his marriage to Anna Magdalena, Bach wrote special music for the birthday of Duke Christian, celebrated in the form of a great hunting festival. The singers played roles from ancient mythology, including Pales (pronounced *Pahless*) the goddess of flocks and herds. This is her lovely, serene aria, about the free, open-air life of shepherds and their flocks.

Gently flowing

Johann Sebastian Bach

(Germany, 1685–1750)

SARABANDE

(From *The Third English Suite*)

In Bach's time and well into the lifetimes of Mozart and Beethoven, there were close ties between composers and the royal patrons who commissioned musical compositions. Pieces like this sarabande were typical of the dance music written to be performed in princely palaces. This dance is slow, stately and elegant.

Grazioso

Johann Sebastian Bach

(Germany, 1685–1750)

AIR ON A G STRING

A famous Bach tune, this *Air* is taken from *Orchestral Suite No. 3*. It earned the nickname "on a G String" after it was arranged for violin and could be played using only one string, the lowest one, which is tuned to G. Keep the tempo slow and avoid any temptation to rush.

Johann Sebastian Bach

(Germany, 1685–1750)

ARIA

(From *The Goldberg Variations*)

This charming *aria* is the opening of *The Goldberg Variations,* a set of 30 variations based on this piece. It was commissioned by a German count for his court musician, Johann Goldberg. Keep a slow and easy tempo, and gently cradle the melody.

Slowly

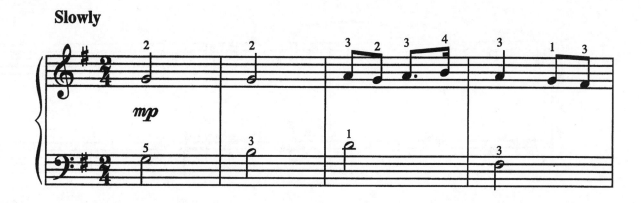

Johann Sebastian Bach

(Germany, 1685–1750)

Tocatta and Fugue in D Minor

(Opening)

This haunting melody is usually heard in old scary movies and at Halloween. Oddly, Bach had no intention of spooking his audience. Rather, this is a short opening to the *Tocatta and Fugue in D Minor* for organ. Note in the middle, your left hand will cross over.

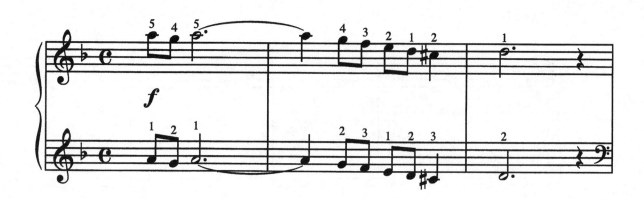

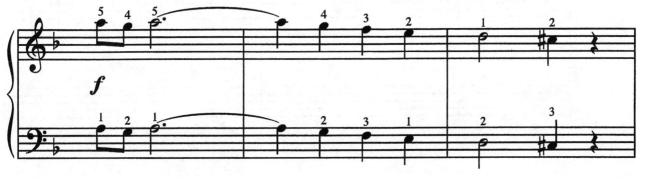

Johann Sebastian Bach

(Germany, 1685–1750)

PRELUDE IN C MAJOR

This charming work is the first prelude from a book called the *Well Tempered Clavier*. It was written to celebrate a new system of tuning keyboard strings that allowed all 12 keys to be performed in tune. Here's a small trick to learning this piece: most of the measures are repeated. Use this chance to look ahead.

Calmly

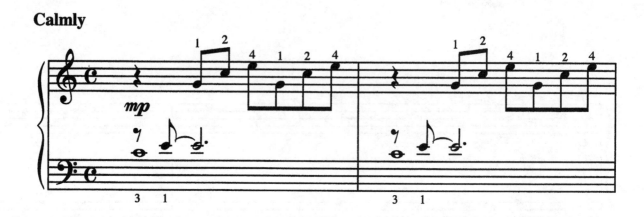

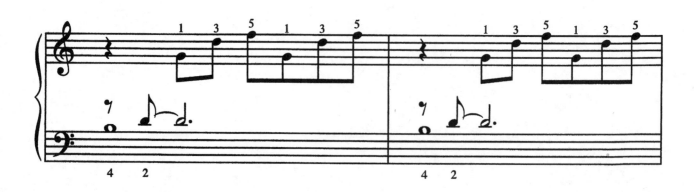

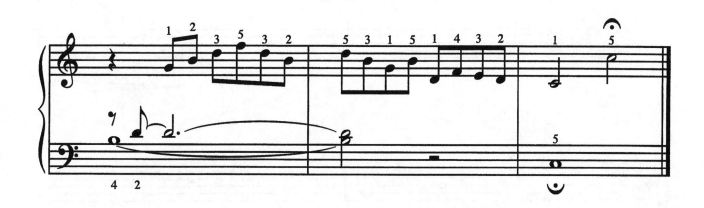

Johann Sebastian Bach

(Germany, 1685–1750)

INVENTION IN F MAJOR

In this piece, Bach makes sure you've been practicing your F major scale and arpeggios. Both hands need to work together to keep the lines smooth and even. Locate the passages of imitation, and be sure that they are echoed properly.

Not Too Fast

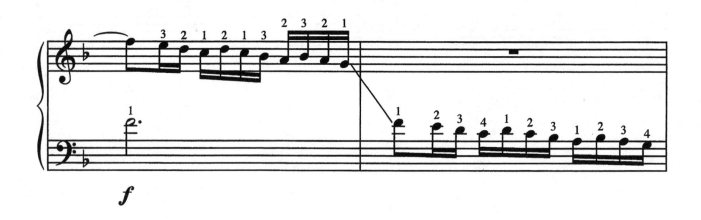

Johann Sebastian Bach

(Germany, 1685–1750)

JESU, JOY OF MAN'S DESIRING

This famous tune is taken from a cantata entitled "Heart and Mouth and Deed and Life" and was first performed on July 2, 1723. Notice that there are many shifts in fingers and repeated notes. This makes it easier to play the next phrase by having your hand in position before your fingers play the note.

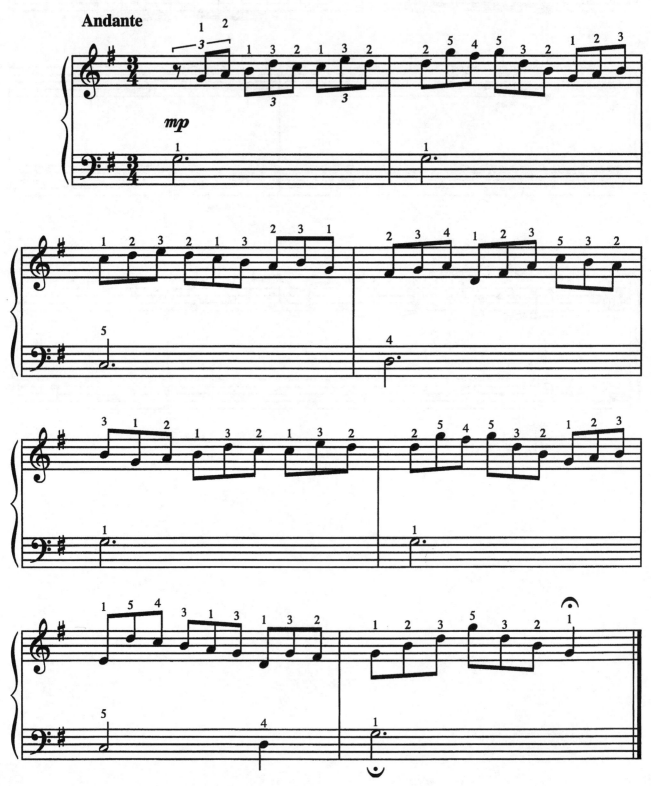

Béla Bartók

(Hungary, 1881–1945)

RUMANIAN SKETCH

Composer Béla Bartók was one of the most diligent researchers of the folk music of Hungary, Rumania, Bulgaria, and other Middle European countries. Notebook and a primitive portable recording machine in hand (there was no electricity in those rustic farmlands!), he jotted down the wonderfully colorful and complicated music he heard. In its melody and rhythms, this sketch is a typical sample of those fascinating sounds.

13

Ludwig van Beethoven

(Germany, 1770–1827)

FÜR ELISE

This famous work was written around 1810. It is thought that Beethoven wrote it to a lost love. Connect the notes in the left hand with those in the right as smoothly as possible to keep the music beautifully flowing.

Moderato

15

Ludwig van Beethoven

(Germany, 1770–1827)

ODE TO JOY

In the year 1822—exactly 100 years after Bach composed his gentle minuet for Anna (see p. 1)—Beethoven solved the troublesome problem of how to end his colossal Symphony No. 9. It would be a musical setting for full chorus of "Ode to Joy," a poem by Friedrich Schiller: *"Joy, we are under your divine spell. All men become brothers wherever joy is found . . ."*

Ludwig van Beethoven

(Germany, 1770–1827)

SONATINA IN G

(Opening)

A *sonatina* is a shorter version of a *sonata,* and usually has two brief movements as opposed to three longer ones. This endearing work was composed around 1785, when Beethoven was a teenager. And ever since then, it's been a favorite amongst pianists.

Ludwig van Beethoven

(Germany, 1770–1827)

MOONLIGHT SONATA

(Opening)

This famous music is taken from the opening of Piano Sonata No. 14. Over the years it has gained the nickname "Moonlight." Play it in a slow manner, and once you are comfortable with the notes, add a sustained effect by applying the right pedal with your foot.

Adagio

Ludwig van Beethoven

(Germany, 1770–1827)

MINUET IN G

This charming court dance is one of Beethoven's most famous pieces. Despite his reputation for lengthy, dramatic compositions, the composer was also fond of writing such short dance music as *éccossaises* (in Scottish style), *allemandes* (in German style), and country dances called *Ländler* and *contredanses*. He composed the Minuet in G about 1795, when he was 25 years old.

Andantino

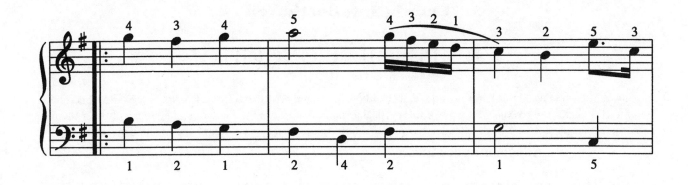

Ludwig van Beethoven

(Germany, 1770–1827)

"EMPEROR" CONCERTO

(Theme from Piano Concerto No. 5)

No one knows who tacked this imposing title on to Beethoven's magnificent Piano Concerto No. 5 in E♭. But it certainly befits a work that is the crowning example of this musical form. In contrast to the thunder and lightning of other themes from this masterpiece, this excerpt is tender, lyrical and almost "vocal" in the way it sings its lovely long melody.

Adagio un poco mosso

Ludwig van Beethoven

(Germany, 1770–1827)

SYMPHONY NO. 5

(Opening)

This is the most famous of all of Beethoven's compositions, if not of all music. It was premiered in 1808 at an all-Beethoven concert, with Beethoven himself conducting. Note that the melody (e.g. measure 5) begins in the right hand and continues into the left—try to make it as smooth as possible.

Allegro con brio

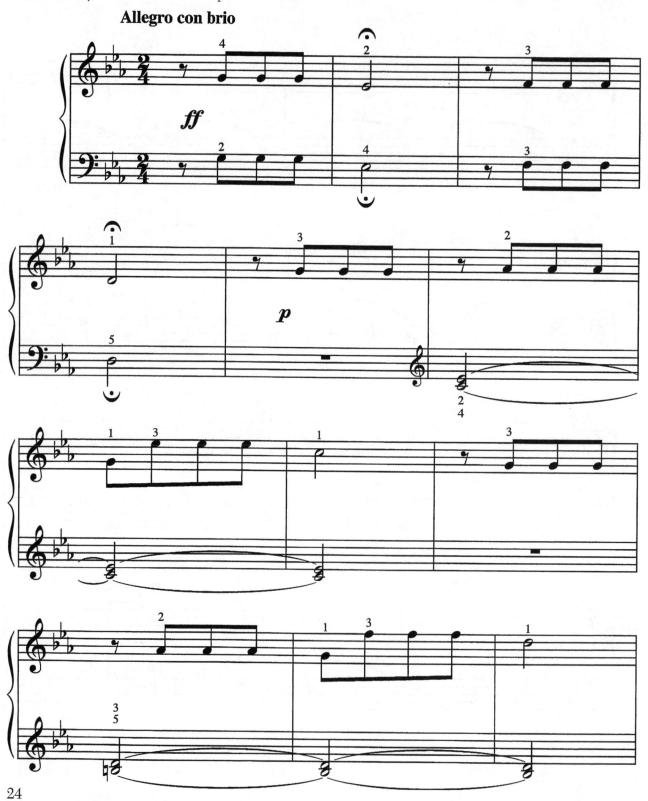

Ludwig van Beethoven

(Germany, 1770–1827)

TURKISH MARCH

In Beethoven's times, Turkish culture was considered exotic and became popular. Musically, composers would adopt such Turkish instruments as cymbals and use them in marches for an effect. When you play this march, try to imagine cymbals clanging in the background.

Allegretto

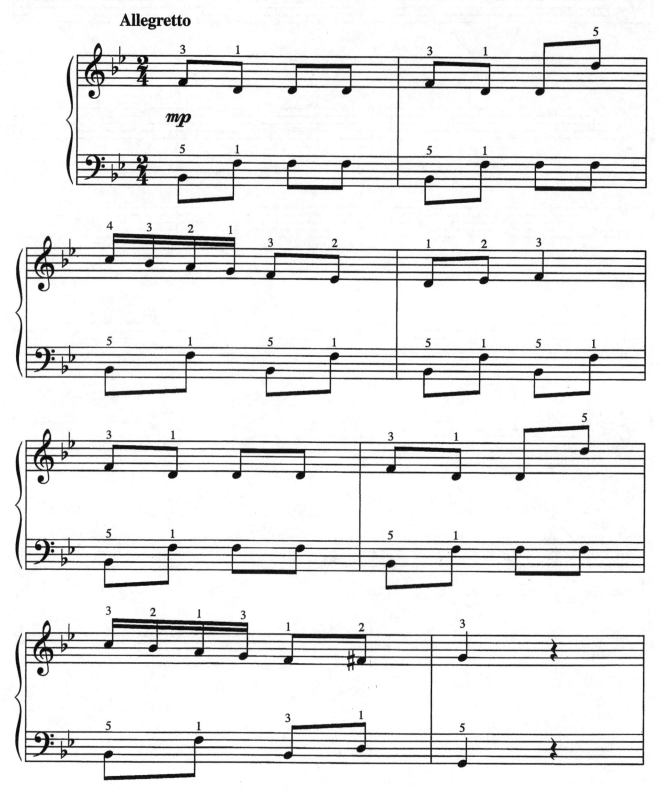

27

Johannes Brahms

(Germany, 1833–1897)

HUNGARIAN DANCE NO. 5

In 1848, when he was 15, a stream of Hungarian rebels passed through Brahm's hometown of Hamburg on their way to America. Some stayed on, bringing their music with them, starting a national craze for the wild, passionate music of the Hungarian Gypsies. Four years later, Brahms began to compose 21 Hungarian Dances, recalling those wonderful tunes and rhythms.

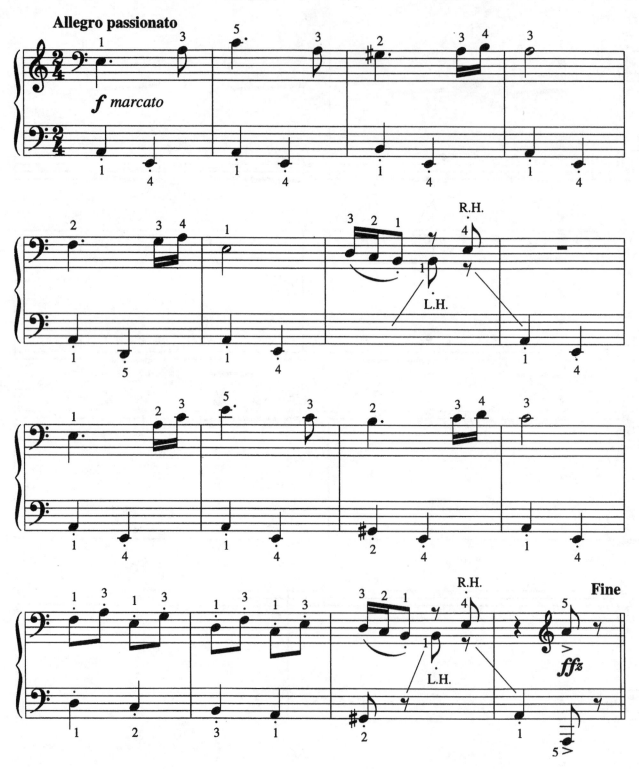

A little slower and lyrical

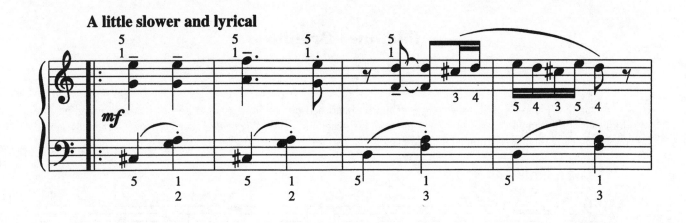

gradually slower _ _ _ _ _ _ _ _ _ _ _

held back, lingering and sentimental _ _ _ _ _ _ _ _   *a tempo*

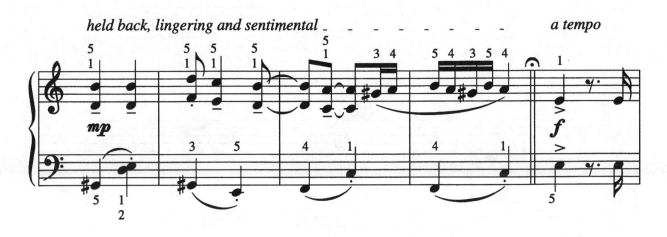

D.C. al Fine

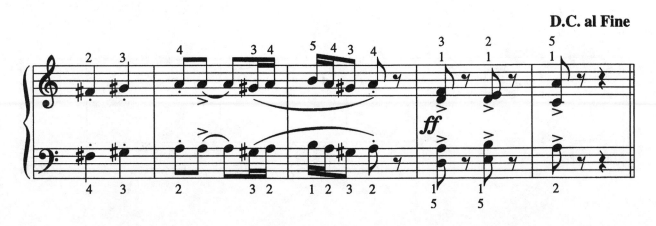

<h1 style="text-align:center">Johannes Brahms</h1>

(Germany, 1833–1897)

<h1 style="text-align:center">LULLABY</h1>

How odd it is that Johannes Brahms—who never married and had no children—should be best known throughout the world for one of the simplest pieces he ever composed: his sweet and gentle *Wiegenlied* (Cradle Song)—originally scored for voice and piano, then later arranged for solo piano.

Andante

Frédéric Chopin

(Poland and France, 1810–1849)

MAZURKA

(Op. 67, No. 2)

"Mazurka" is a title that comes from the name *mazurek,* a dance from the Polish province of Mazovia. Chopin, born in Poland, recalls for us this fascinating dance form—sometimes as a lively, heavily accented folk piece, but here as a melancholy, plaintive memory of his homeland. The Italian tempo marking *cantabile* tells us to play the music in a "singing" fashion—flowing and lyrical.

Cantabile

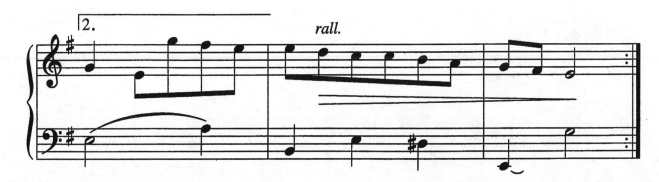

Frédéric Chopin

(Poland and France, 1810–1849)

NOCTURNE

Piano composers in the 19th century were fond of giving fanciful, often meaningless, names to their pieces—such as "rhapsody," "impromptu," "album leaf," "intermezzo," "fantasy" and so on. Chopin liked the French word "nocturne" (night piece) for 21 piano pieces composed in a dreamy mood. This one (Opus 9, No. 2) is his most famous nocturne, full of beautiful melody.

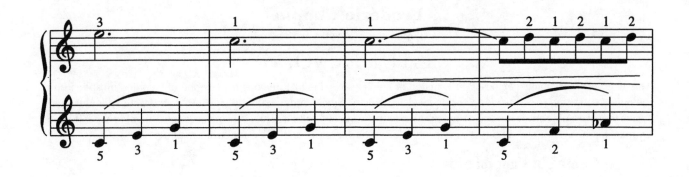

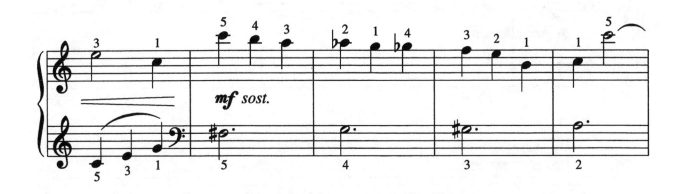

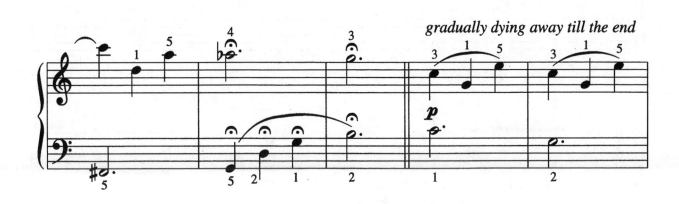

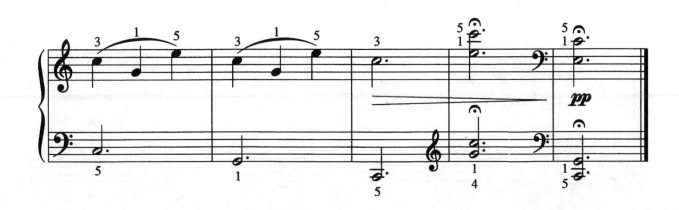

Frédéric Chopin

(Poland and France, 1810–1849)

ETUDE NO. 3

This Etude was originally composed in E major, in 2/4. This version in F major presents one of Chopin's most beautiful melodies, known all over the world for its lovely simplicity. Since *étude* [AYE-tood] means "a study," this famous piece seems to be Chopin's study in a full, "singing" tone at the keyboard, with a gently rocking accompaniment in the left hand. Our version in 4/4 doubles all the original note values (quarters instead of 8ths) for easier reading.

Gently, but not too slow

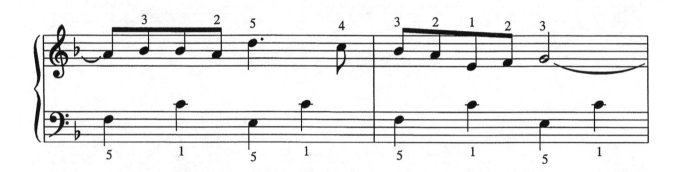

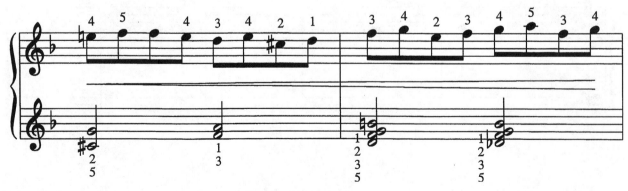

34

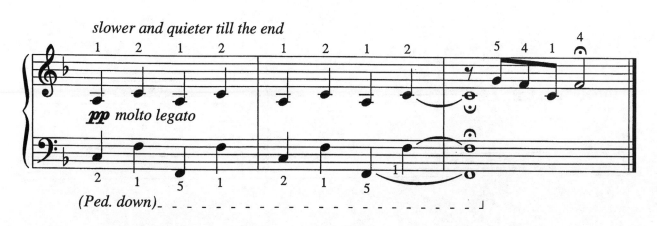

Frédéric Chopin

(Poland and France, 1810–1849)

PRELUDE NO. 7

Among Chopin's works, the title "Prelude" has no special meaning. Of his 24 pieces with this title, some are sketches barely a minute long; others are quite developed and theatrical. With its two-measure rhythm played *eight* times, Prelude No. 7 presents a challenge to shape the music in an interesting way, with varying "dynamics" (degrees of loud and soft) as you move from phrase to phrase.

Andantino

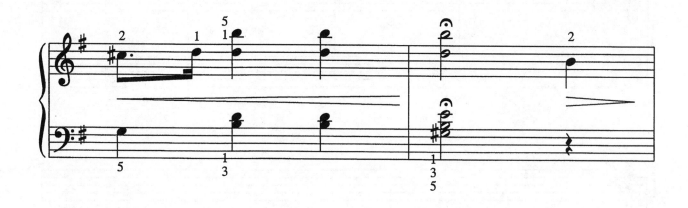

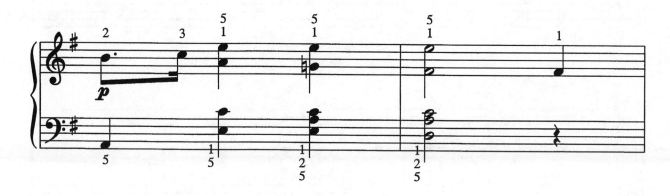

rall. _ _ _ _ _ _ _ _ _ _ _ _ _ _ _ _ _ molto

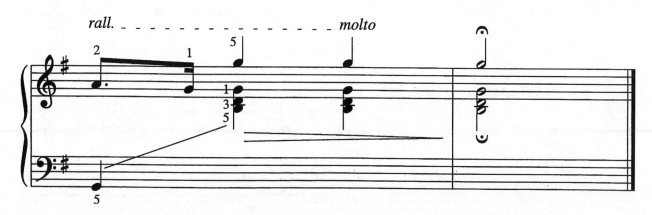

Frédéric Chopin

(Poland and France, 1810–1849)

FUNERAL MARCH

The third movement of Chopin's Sonata No. 2, Op. 35. Despite the tempo marking, don't drag this familiar piece to death! Keep the rhythm steady, moving along at a gentle pace. Notice that the left hand *never* changes; once you learn the fingering, you've got nothing more to think about! Then give some shape to the music: perhaps it could start and end very softly, but build in the middle—as though the procession began far, far away, came nearer, then disappeared.

Slow and heavy

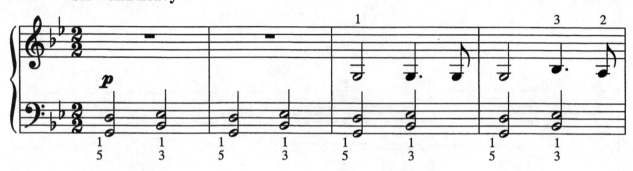

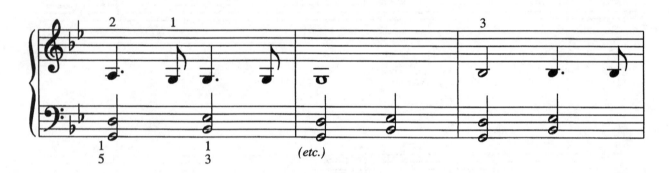

(etc.)

gradually dying away till the end

Frédéric Chopin

(Poland and France, 1810–1849)

"RAINDROP" PRELUDE

The theme of Prelude in D-flat, Op. 28 no. 15, here in D major. Those repeated A's in the left hand are supposed to imitate raindrops, but no one really knows what was on Chopin's mind when he composed this music. For the best performance, play that lovely right-hand melody very smoothly (*legato*) and sweetly (*dolce*), while your left hand intones those A's in the background, quietly and lightly detached (*piano e poco leggiero*). <u>Practice hands separately!</u>

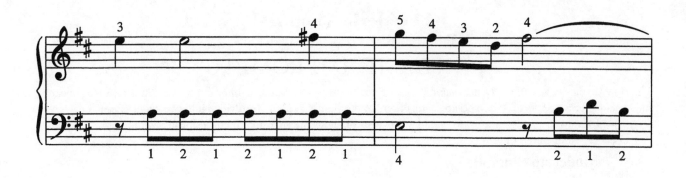

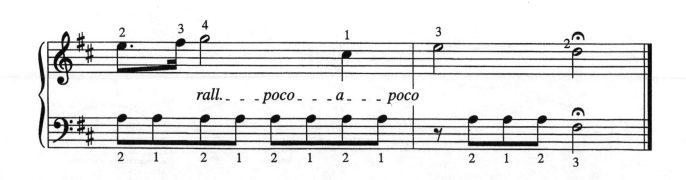

Frédéric Chopin

(Poland and France, 1810–1849)

FANTAISIE-IMPROMPTU

The slow theme—originally in D-flat major, here in F major, from the Fantaisie-impromptu, Op. 66. And what a beauti-fully balanced musical form!—16 measures altogether (count them) . . . perfectly divided into two pages . . . each page per-fectly divided into four little phrases. As you play this world-famous music, listen to how effortlessly it unfolds . . . expands . . . repeats . . . and comes to rest.

Moderato cantabile

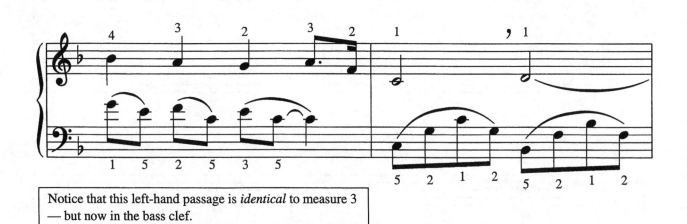

Notice that this left-hand passage is *identical* to measure 3 — but now in the bass clef.

rall. _ _ _ _ _ poco _ _ _ _ _ a _ _ _ _ poco

Muzio Clementi

(Italy, 1752–1832)

AIR SUISSE

(Swiss Tune from Sonata, Op. 36, No. 5)

In one amazing lifetime, Muzio Clementi had the most varied set of professions one can imagine. He was a piano virtuoso, teacher, conductor, composer, publisher and piano manufacturer! Traveling throughout Europe and Russia, he even found time to perform in a piano contest before European royalty! Who was his opponent? None other than Wolfgang Amadeus Mozart himself!

Light and airy

poco rall.

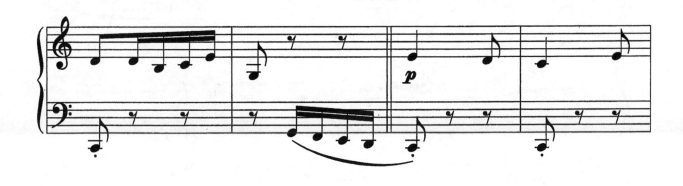

poco rall. _ _ _ _ _ _ _ _ _ _ _ _ _

45

Muzio Clementi

(Italy, 1752–1832)

RONDO IN C

(From Sonata in C, Op. 36, No. 1)

Muzio Clementi is recognized as the first composer to write specifically for the piano. He is best known for his collection of 110 piano sonatas. This Rondo is taken from his Sonata in C, Op. 36, No. 1, Clementi's most recognizable work.

Claude Debussy

(France, 1862–1918)

THE MAIDEN WITH THE FLAXEN HAIR

(No. 8 of twelve Preludes, Book I)

In the original publication of this piece, the composer placed the title at the end of the music rather than in its usual position at the start! In this way, Debussy seems to be telling us to think of the music first, then look at its "label" as an afterthought. Either way, we like to "paint" this piece as a gentle sound-portrait—songful and restrained.

Antonín Dvořák

(Czechoslovakia, 1841–1904)

FROM THE NEW WORLD

(Slow theme from the second movement of Symphony No. 9, Op. 95)

Dvořák was 51 when he was invited to America as director of a New York music conservatory. He arrived with his family for a three-year stay, spending their summers in a Czech community in Iowa. There, in 1893, he completed his Symphony "From the New World." The song "Goin' Home," with words by William Arms Fisher (1922), was based on Dvořák's original slow theme for the second movement. It was not a Negro spiritual, as some people believed.

Antonín Dvořák

(Czechoslovakia, 1841–1904)

HUMORESQUE

(Op. 101, No. 7)

Not many people know that this world-famous music comes from a collection of no fewer than eight "humoresques" originally published as a set of piano pieces. The popularity of this particular one comes from its charming dance-like feeling, offered in a recipe for easy listening: a pretty tune with a catchy rhythm repeated throughout. With their easy-to-find locations on the keyboard, all those black keys should make playing even easier than usual!

Gracefully, not too fast

(slightly held back)

Stephen C. Foster

(United States, 1826–1864)

BEAUTIFUL DREAMER

In a life cut tragically short (he died in poverty at age 37), Stephen Collins Foster wrote about 200 songs. Many are so well-known, and have been around for such a long time, that we think of them as genuine folk songs. His famous "My Old Kentucky Home" became the official state song of Kentucky, and his beloved "Old Folks at Home" was chosen as Florida's state song.

Christoph Willibald Gluck
(Austria and France, 1714–1787)
BALLET AIR
(From the opera *Orfeo ed Euridice*)

An occasional ballet was always a delightful moment in the course of an opera—and this delicate "air" from such a ballet gives us a good idea of the melodious music heard by its enchanted audience. Play it in a restrained way, with a gentle movement. First, play the music from beginning to end. When you get to "D.C. al Fine" (abbreviation for the Italian *da capo al fine*—"from head to end") return to the beginning of the music, then play right up to the "Fine"—but no further!

Edvard Grieg

(Norway, 1843–1907)

PIANO CONCERTO

(Lyrical theme from Finale)

Did you know that Grieg brought the manuscript of his marvelous concerto to none other than the great Franz Liszt for a frank critique? The master sight-read the score, praising the young composer with wonderfully encouraging words. Grieg's concerto went on to great acclaim, with hundreds of performances worldwide every year! Play this lovely theme— a memorable moment in the composition—with a gently flowing feeling, letting the ending vanish away.

Tranquillo

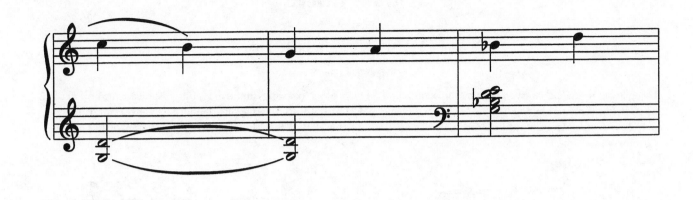

Edvard Grieg

(Norway, 1843–1907)

MORNING MOOD

(From *Peer Gynt*)

Grieg loved his native Norway, pouring the sounds and feelings of its folk songs and dances into his music. At the age of 31, Grieg was invited by the famous Norwegian playwright Henrik Ibsen to write "incidental" music to accompany his play *Peer Gynt*. "Morning Mood," "Anitra's Dance" and "In the Hall of the Mountain King" are three world-famous selections from that fine music.

George Frideric Handel

(Germany and England, 1685–1759)

SARABANDE

Did you know that Johann Sebastian Bach, Domenico Scarlatti and Handel were all born in the same year (1685)? All three were not only great composers, but phenomenal keyboard virtuosos as well. They wrote and performed some of the greatest, most popular harpsichord music ever composed. This stately court dance is from Handel's Suite in D minor for harpsichord, published in 1720.

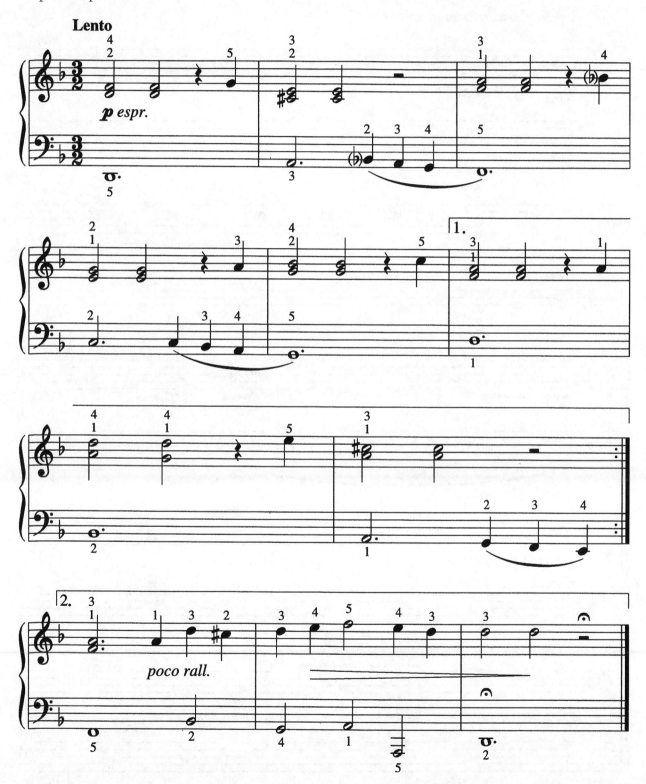

George Frideric Handel

(Germany and England, 1685–1759)

THE HARMONIOUS BLACKSMITH

(Air from *The Fifth Harpsichord Suite*)

Here is the beginning of an Air with Variations from the great master's Harpsichord Suite No. 5. No one knows for sure where the title came from—perhaps from an obscure folktune, perhaps tacked on by a publisher in need of a catchy idea to sell copies of the music. Pay attention to the abrupt changes of dynamics and play the piece with hearty good spirits.

Moderato, in good spirits

Joseph Haydn

(Austria, 1732–1809)

SONATA IN C

(First movement of Sonata No. 35)

History says that young Haydn was a lively boy who loved practical jokes. As a young man, however, he had a hard time supporting himself—teaching a bit, performing a lot, and composing continually to make a living. Today, he is honored as "father" of the classical sonata and the symphony . . . and his list of works fills over 40 pages of the music encyclopedia!

Joseph Haydn
(Austria, 1732–1809)
RONDO

"Papa" Haydn lived to the ripe age of 77—a rarity in the 18th century—and few composers have found the time or energy to compose as much music. As part of his vast output, he wrote 104 symphonies, 85 string quartets, 31 trios, and 52 keyboard sonatas and partitas! This sprightly rondo—characterized by frequent returns to its main theme—is the finale of his thirty-fifth piano sonata.

Joseph Haydn

(Austria, 1732–1809)

"SURPRISE" SYMPHONY

The popular story goes that Haydn wanted "to wake up the ladies" by shocking his audience with an unexpected drum stroke played *forte*. This "surprise" occurs in the otherwise peaceful slow movement of his Symphony No. 94. This tuneful work is one of the composer's so-called "London" symphonies—twelve works written for concerts he gave in London, from 1791 to 1795.

Franz Liszt

(Hungary and Germany, 1811–1886)

CONSOLATION

Based on one of Liszt's most beautiful themes, this enchanting music should be played quietly and unhurried, with a gentle touch. Pay special attention to the left-hand chords that support the melody from start to finish. Play these harmonies so that all of the chord is heard, with each of its three or four notes quietly but firmly balanced. Of special interest and importance is the low sound on the first beat of each measure. Let the pedal sustain that sound as long as possible.

Lento placido

smooth, unhurried

p *floating freely*

(a distant echo)

pp

gradually dying away _

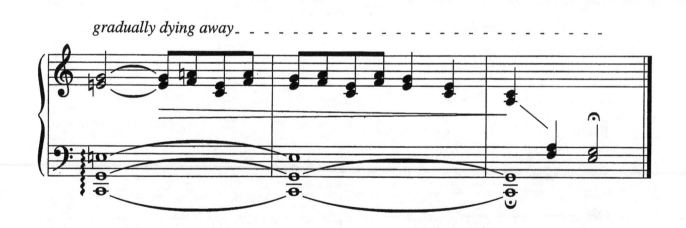

Franz Liszt

(Hungary and Germany, 1811–1886)

HUNGARIAN RHAPSODY NO. 2

Liszt was *the* great superstar of the 19th century. Considered by some to be the best pianist who ever lived, he was honored by kings and adored by the public who flocked to his sold-out concerts throughout Europe and Russia. They especially loved to hear Liszt play his own pieces based on the sad tunes and wild dances of the gypsy bands that traveled throughout his native Hungary.

64

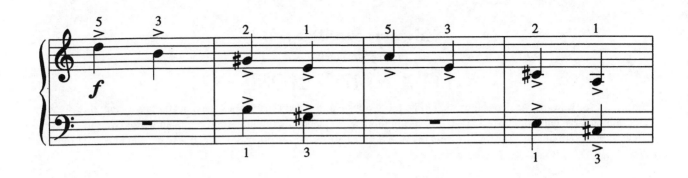

gradually pulling back, bigger and broader

Edward MacDowell

(United States, 1860–1908)

TO A WILD ROSE

The American Edward MacDowell was a lot like the Norwegian Edvard Grieg. They lived at the same time, they were both fine pianists, and both were at their best writing miniature pieces about nature and homeland. MacDowell's gentle "To a Wild Rose," composed in 1896, is from his *Woodland Sketches*. Three other popular suites are called *Fireside Tales*, *New England Idylls*, and *Sea Pieces*.

Wolfgang Amadeus Mozart

(Austria, 1756–1791)

MINUET

(From *Don Giovanni*)

A minuet is a slow and stately dance in 3/4 time. This minuet is from one of Mozart's most famous operas, *Don Giovanni*. The characters all dance onstage at the end of Act I to this lovely melody.

Moderato

Wolfgang Amadeus Mozart

(Austria, 1756–1791)

PAPAGENO'S SONG

You may think opera is stuffy—but then you haven't heard Mozart's fairy-tale "singing play" called *The Magic Flute*! It has a prince, a girl he has to rescue, a wizard, a magic flute, and a comical birdcatcher called Papageno. "Yes, I am the birdcatcher," he sings, "always cheerful, well-known everywhere! If only I could catch a sweet young girl so that she'd be all mine! I'd feed her on sugar!"

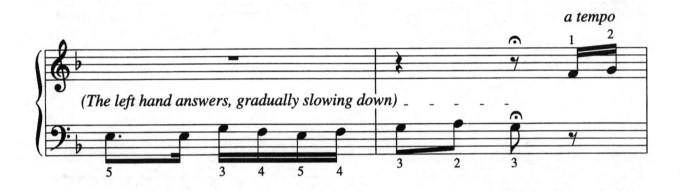

(The right hand tells its own story) _ _ _ _ _ _ _ _

a tempo

(The left hand answers, gradually slowing down) _ _ _ _ _ _

(a light-hearted duet)

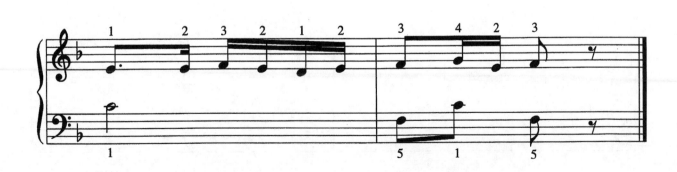

Wolfgang Amadeus Mozart

(Austria, 1756–1791)

ROMANZE

"Romanze" is the German spelling of *romance*—in music, the name for a gentle and lyrical piece that is very melodious, with a tender character. This *Romanze* is the slow movement of Mozart's popular Piano Concerto No. 20. Did you know that this great composer (who lived over 200 years ago) was also a wonderful pianist? He first performed in public at the age of 5—and could even play blindfolded!

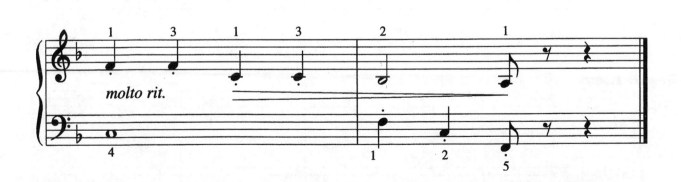

Wolfgang Amadeus Mozart

(Austria, 1756–1791)

SONATA IN A

(Theme from Piano Sonata, K331)

This is the world-famous main theme from one of the six piano sonatas Mozart composed at the age of twenty-two. Unbelievably, this great master left a legacy of more than 600 compositions before he died so tragically at the age of thirty-five—including works for every chamber-music ensemble then available to him, a host of concertos for piano and for every principal instrument of the orchestra, and no fewer than forty-one symphonies! The greatest tribute to Mozart's mastery is the fact that every one of his important works—including seven major operas—is still performed frequently throughout the world.

Andante grazioso

poco rall.

Wolfgang Amadeus Mozart

(Austria, 1756–1791)

ALLEGRO

(From *Eine Kleine Nachtmusik*)

This is the opening to one of Mozart's most famous works, *Eine Kleine Nachtmusik,* which means "A Little Night Music." It was composed in 1787 while Mozart was living in Vienna. Be sure to keep the music light and flowing.

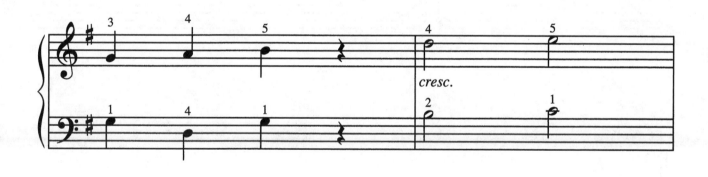

Wolfgang Amadeus Mozart

(Austria, 1756–1791)

ARIA

(From *Don Giovanni*)

Here's another piece from the famous opera *Don Giovanni,* this time an aria. Sung by a solo voice, an aria allows a character to express their thoughts and feelings uninterrupted. Feel free to hum or sing along!

Andante

Wolfgang Amadeus Mozart

(Austria, 1756–1791)

OVERTURE

(To *The Marriage of Figaro*)

An overture is an introduction to an opera, where the main themes are introduced and the story is outlined—much like a movie trailer. This overture is from *The Marriage of Figaro,* where the story plays like a soap opera. Figaro is set to marry his love Susanna only to have an old count return and try to steal her away. The overture sets the tone for this lively story.

Presto

Wolfgang Amadeus Mozart

(Austria, 1756–1791)

Rondo Alla Turca

(From Piano Sonata No. 11)

This well-known melody is from the third movement of the *Piano Sonata No. 11*. The notes can be a bit tricky, but be sure to keep a nice and even pace and contrast the *piano* and *forte* sections.

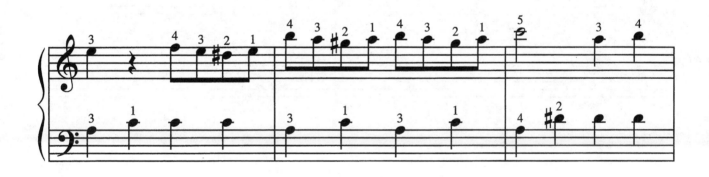

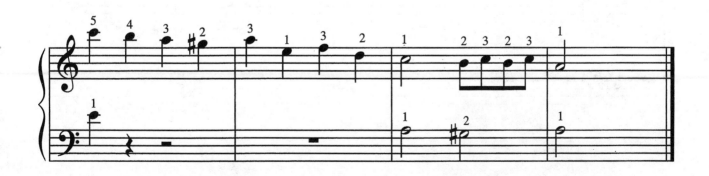

Wolfgang Amadeus Mozart

(Austria, 1756–1791)

SYMPHONY NO. 40

(Opening)

Of his last three symphonies, the middle one, symphony no. 40, is the best known. Although most of Mozart's compositions were usually composed on commission—for concerts, or as gifts for his friends—there is no record of Mozart having received any commission or payment for this symphony. It is believed he wrote it in hopes of selling it, or presenting it in concert, but no one can be sure—it was not published until after his death.

Allegro molto

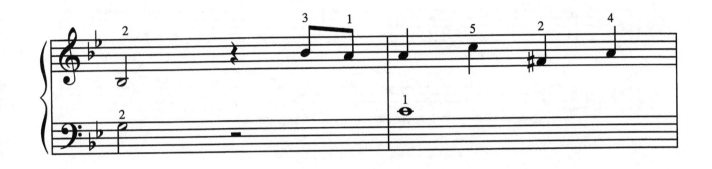

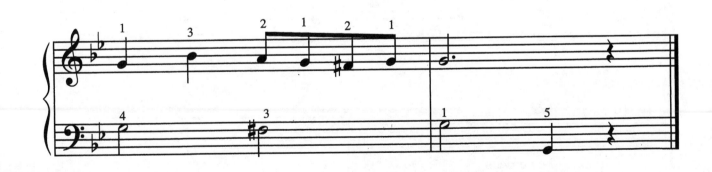

Felix Mendelssohn

(Germany and England, 1809–1847)

VENETIAN GONDOLA SONG

Felix Mendelssohn wrote a number of lyrical short piano pieces he called *Songs Without Words,* including such well-known compositions as "Spring Song" and "The Spinning Wheel." As we can easily imagine, this "Venetian Boat Song" captures the two elements we anticipate in such music: in the left hand, the endless flow of gentle water beneath the boat; in the right hand, the plaintive song of the gondolier, characterized by the sweet melancholy of its melody.

Allegretto tranquillo

Modest Mussorgsky
(Russia, 1839–1881)
HOPAK

The *hopak* (or *gopak*) is a lively dance that originated in the section of Russia called Byelorussia (Little Russia). With its strong two-beat feeling, the hopak is characterized by heavy accents to accompany a kind of stamping dance so popular among villagers throughout Europe and Asia. Our example sits almost entirely on the piano's black keys. Remember to observe all those repeat signs on the first page of this arrangement.

A lively stamping dance

hold back just a little

Ignacy Jan Paderewski

(Poland, 1860–1941)

KRAKOWIAK

(Polish Dance, Op. 5, No. 1)

Like the preceding *hopak,* this dance originated as a popular village dance—in this instance, from the town of Krakow in Poland. The music is always in 2/4 time and uses strong accents and simple syncopations. The *krakowiak* was always danced by large groups, accompanied by shouting, improvised singing, and striking of the heels together. Especially popular in the early nineteenth century, a wonderful example of its style and spirit has come down to us today in Chopin's marvelous Krakowiak for piano and orchestra.

Lively, playful

Tempo I

hold back a little

Ignacy Jan Paderewski

(Poland, 1860–1941)

MINUET IN OLDEN STYLE

Can you imagine a superstar music celebrity becoming *head* of the country? Strange as it seems, that's what happened to pianist-composer Ignacy Paderewski at the age of 59. Using his worldwide reputation as a great performer, he raised money for Polish victims of World War I and for Polish liberation. In 1919, he became Poland's Prime Minister and helped sign the Treaty of Versailles that ended the war. Paderewski played this extremely popular, very charming Minuet all over the world.

Jean-Philippe Rameau

(France, 1683–1764)

TAMBOURIN

Rameau was composing in France when America was still a group of colonies governed by the King of England. Although he wrote 33 little operas and ballets, and many miniatures for harpsichord (the "grandfather" of the modern piano), he was proudest of his many books on music theory. The *tambourin* of this lively piece was a long, narrow drum from southern France, near Spain. It is *not* a tambourine!

Serge Rachmaninoff

(Russia and United States, 1873–1943)

PRELUDE

Some call this mighty Prelude by the name "The Bells of Moscow." Those powerful left-hand tones—long and accented—do suggest the tolling of large church bells. But notice that the right-hand "echoes" are always subdued and plaintive, like a quiet afterthought. Although Rachmaninoff wrote 24 Preludes, this is the one his worldwide audiences demanded at every piano recital he played. This popular composer-pianist lived till the age of 69, but wrote this piece when he was only 20 years old.

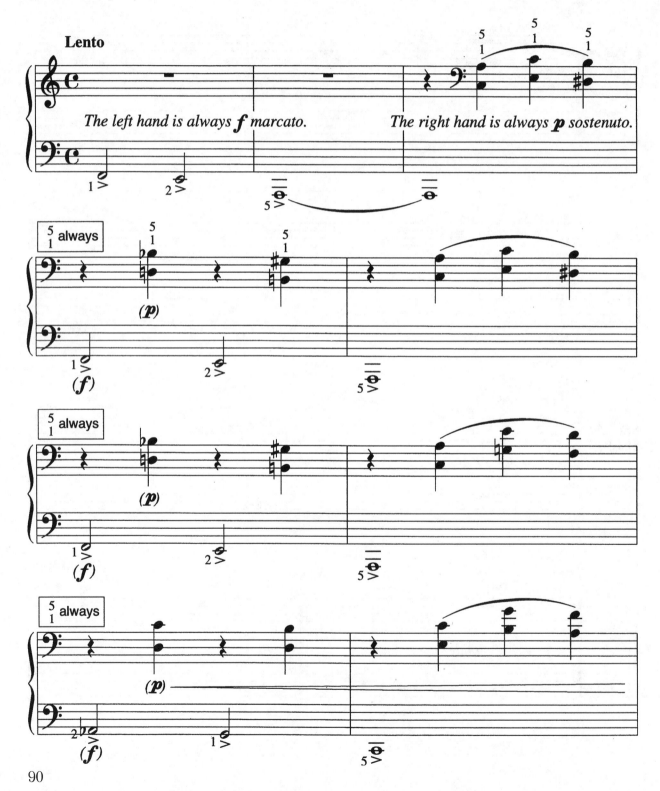

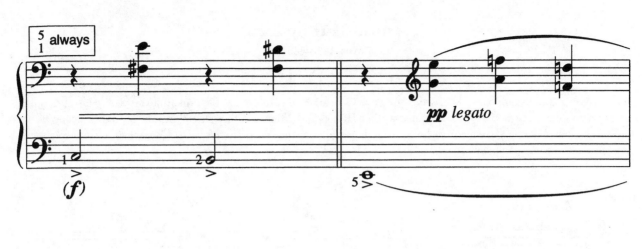

Anton Rubinstein

(Russia, 1829–1894)

MELODY IN F

Some say that Rubinstein looked like a lion, but played like an angel. He lived at the same time as the great Franz Liszt, and was considered *almost* as great a pianist as that Hungarian virtuoso. Although Rubinstein composed many piano pieces and five mighty piano concertos, he is remembered almost exclusively for this simple *Melody in F.* Some know the tune as the song "Welcome, Sweet Springtime."

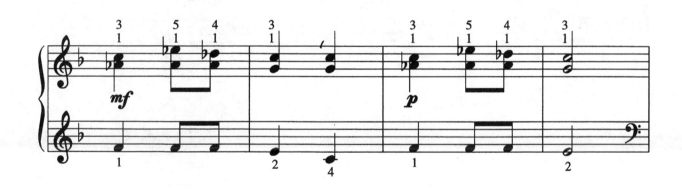

rall. - - poco - - a - - poco

D.C. al Fine

93

Camille Saint-Saëns

(France, 1835–1921)

THE SWAN

Intended as a musical joke, Saint-Saëns' *The Carnival of the Animals* was dashed off in a few days while the composer was on vacation in February 1886. "The Swan" was always a highlight of the 14 pieces he called his "grand zoological fantasy." Notice how it perfectly captures the feeling of an elegant swan floating on a still lake. (Pronounce this French composer's name *ka-mee san-sawn*.)

poco rit. - - - - - - - - - - - - *a tempo*

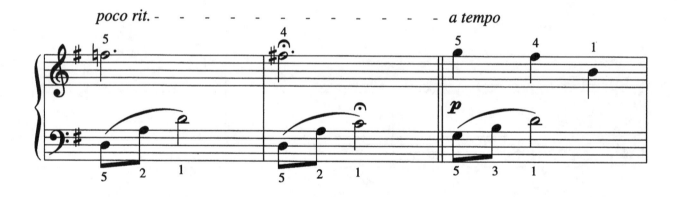

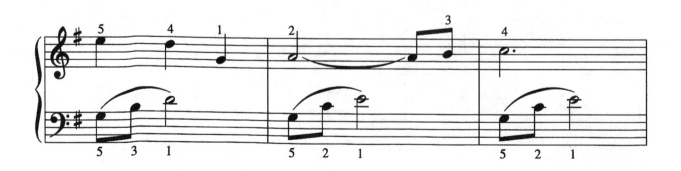

96

gradually relaxing until the quiet end

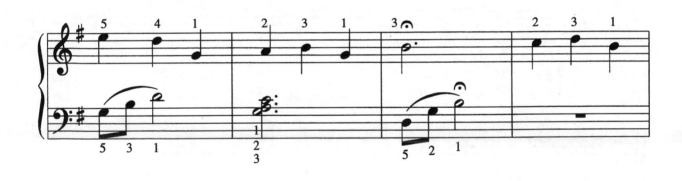

Erik Satie

(France, 1866–1925)

LULLABY

(From *Picturesque Child's Play*; original edition)

You can always depend on the French composer Erik Satie to come up with something that no one else has thought of! This time it is a quiet lullaby accompanied by a running bedtime conversation between a little boy and his mother. (Maybe Satie has the right idea after all, helping us to interpret his odd music.) Notice how your two hands play a kind of duet as they move from phrase to phrase—with quarter-note motion first in one hand, then in the other.

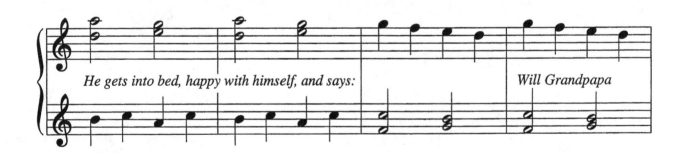

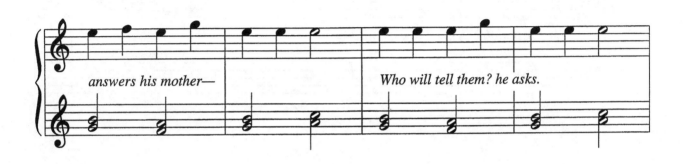

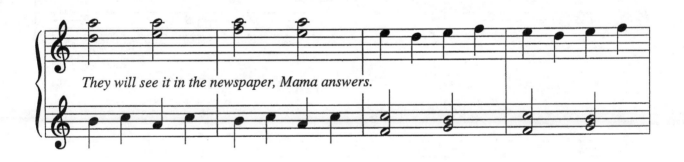

Domenico Scarlatti

(Italy, 1685–1757)

Sonata in D Minor

(Aria)

Born the same year as Johann Sebastian Bach, Domenico Scarlatti brought something new to keyboard music—a set of more than 500 miniature keyboard "sonatas" brilliantly colored by their elegant, decorative, swift virtuoso style. "When we hear Scarlatti's music," a great pianist once said, "we know we are in the climate of sunlight and warmth, of Italy, Spain and the spirit of the Latin countries." Scarlatti labeled his little gems with various titles: *pastorale . . . tarantella . . . Sicilienne.* This one is *"Aria,"* characterized by its song-like melody and charming simplicity.

Andantino

poco rit.   *a tempo*

poco rall.

Franz Schubert

(Austria, 1797–1828)

THE TROUT

"The Trout" was originally a short poem about a hasty fish about to be hooked by a patient fisherman. Schubert loved this verse so much that he first set it to music as a song for voice and piano. Two years later, at age 22, he borrowed his own melody for a "theme-and-variations" movement composed for piano, violin, viola, cello and string bass. Naturally, this famous piece is called the "Trout" Quintet.

Coda: *slightly slower*

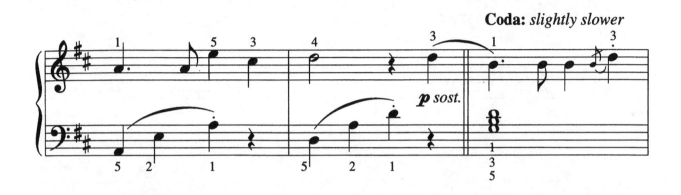

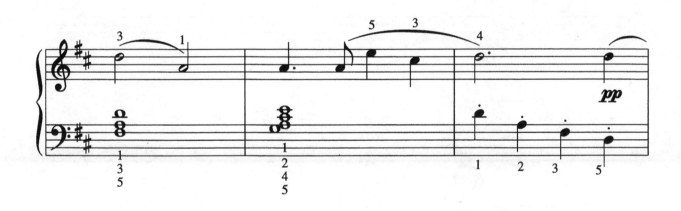

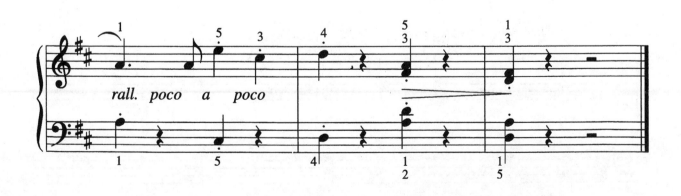

Franz Schubert

(Austria, 1797–1828)

IMPROMPTU

(Op. 142, No. 2)

The title "impromptu" has no special musical meaning, joining the group of meaningless names thought up by the nineteenth-century Romantics to identify their music. This one joins the ranks of such fanciful labels as "rhapsody," "album leaf," "intermezzo," "fantasy," "nocturne," and so on. Schubert's lovely Impromptu—tender and straightforward—needs nothing more than a simple performance, without exaggerated rhythm or dynamics.

Allegretto

rall. poco a poco

Robert Schumann

(Germany, 1810–1856)

TRÄUMEREI

(From *Scenes from Childhood,* Op. 15)

The fact that Clara and Robert Schumann had *eight* children may have something to do with Robert's devotion to children's music—a rarity among 19th-century composers. He composed his *Album for the Young* for beginning players, and *Scenes from Childhood* for *all* pianists. "Träumerei" means "revery," describing a dreamy movement in a child's life. Play it gently (*dolce*), but without dragging the tempo.

Robert Schumann

(Germany, 1810–1856)

THE HAPPY FARMER

(From *Album for the Young*, Op. 68)

Here's a delightful piece from the suite that Schumann composed for beginning pianists. He finished all 43 miniatures in only two weeks, and gave the first seven pieces to his daughter Marie as a gift for her seventh birthday. The full title of this piece is "The Happy Farmer Returning from Work"—a good clue for playing it. Like the farmer coming home again, it should be full of joy.

Robert Schumann

(Germany, 1810–1856)

THE POET SPEAKS

(From *Scenes from Childhood,* Op. 15)

The Poet Speaks is the last of the 13 pieces that make up Robert Schumann's *Scenes from Childhood*—a collection of picturesque pieces designed to allow pianists to envision childhood through music. This short conclusion is given as a final thought from the composer (the "poet") to the children and all his listeners.

Slow, reflective

Peter Ilyitch Tchaikovsky

(Russia, 1840–1893)

SYMPHONY NO. 6

(Theme)

Tchaikovsky wrote a total of six symphonies. The last one is nicknamed *Pathétique*. Don't rush the tempo, and let the melody gently flow.

Slowly

Peter Ilyitch Tchaikovsky
(Russia, 1840–1893)
MARCHE SLAVE

Tchaikovsky loved the music of the many peoples that lived in and near the vast boundaries of his native Russia. The Slavs were the most numerous of these groups, coming from Russia, Poland, Czechoslovakia, Serbia and other neighboring countries. This *Marche Slave* ('slave' is pronounced *slahv*) means "Slavonic March" and is based on a Serbian folksong.

Slow march

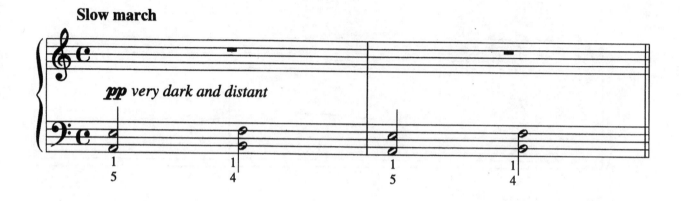

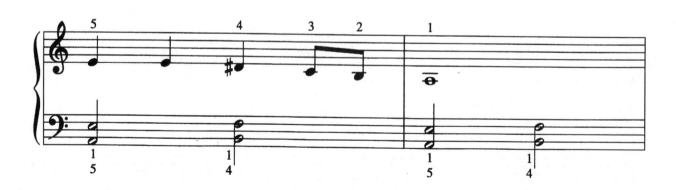

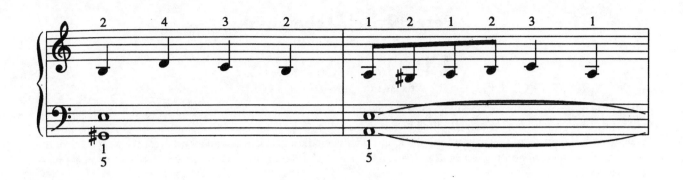

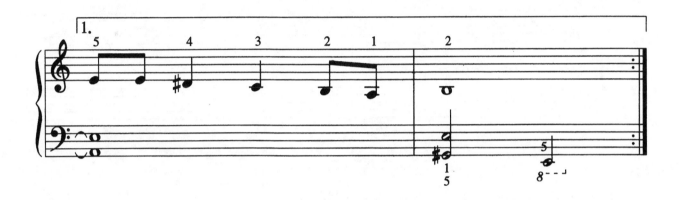

gradually slower till the end, dying away

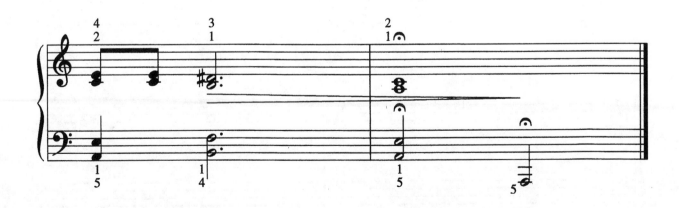

Peter Ilyitch Tchaikovsky

(Russia, 1840–1893)

FIFTH SYMPHONY

(Horn theme from Movement II of Op. 64)

This is one of the most famous themes in all of Tchaikovsky's music. In its original orchestral score, this lovely melody is played by the French horn, bringing to it all of the rich, mellow color typical of this important brass instrument. The melody itself is quite simple, with easy repetitions and slight melodic and rhythmic variations. Treat the long notes of the left hand as a quiet support underneath the theme. As marked, let the ending fade away completely to its final *ppp*—pianississimo.

Andante cantabile

dying away

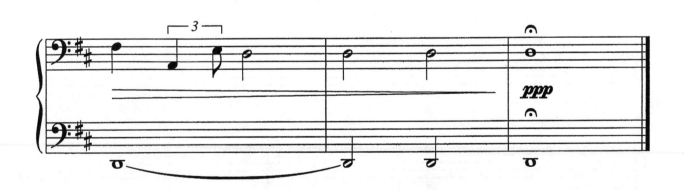

ppp

Peter Ilyitch Tchaikovsky

(Russia, 1840–1893)

ROMEO AND JULIET

(Theme)

Shakespeare has long served to inspire composers, such as Mendelssohn and Verdi. Tchaikovsky wrote an orchestral piece based on the tragic story of *Romeo and Juliet*. You'll find that he used accidentals to portray the emotion of the work, such as the D♭ in the right hand at the end.

Slowly

Peter Ilyitch Tchaikovsky

(Russia, 1840–1893)

1812 OVERTURE

(Allegro)

This famous passage from the *1812 Overture* is synonymous with fireworks and the Fourth of July. Tchaikovsky wrote the work for a huge orchestra—and even wrote a part for real cannons to fire! Keep the tempo festive, and light up the keyboard.

Allegro

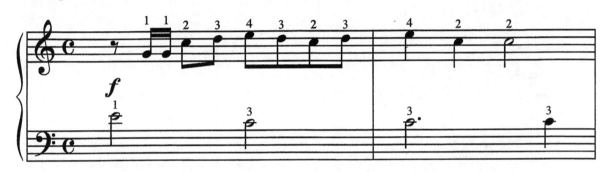

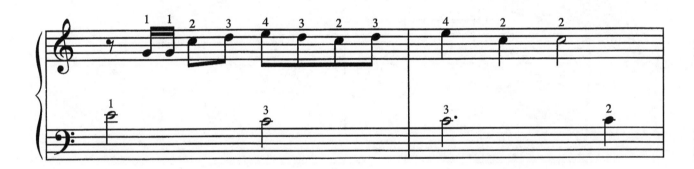

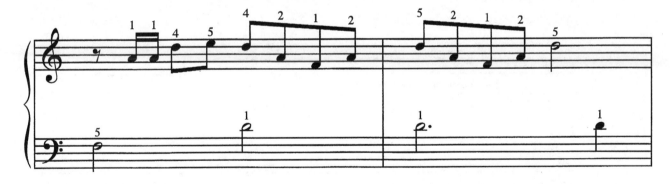

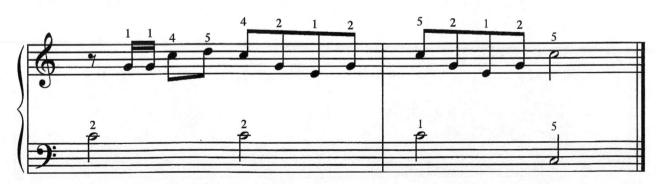

Peter Ilyitch Tchaikovsky
(Russia, 1840–1893)
SWAN LAKE
(Theme)

Swan Lake is a popular ballet that tells the story of Prince Siegfried and his love, Princess Odette. As with many musical tragedies, composers use contrast to show the different sides of the story. Here, the opening theme is tragic and in minor, contrasted by a lighter melody in major on page 117.

Majestic

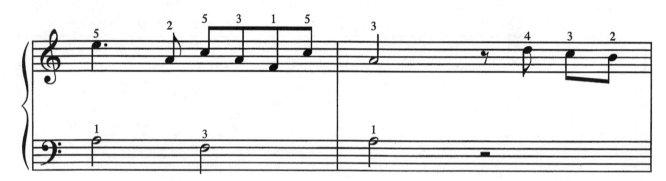

Peter Ilyitch Tchaikovsky
(Russia, 1840–1893)

EUGENE ONEGIN WALTZ

This catchy waltz is taken from the opera *Eugene Onegin*. Be careful not to rush the trickier passages. Practice them slowly and bring them up to speed little by little.

Tempo di Valse

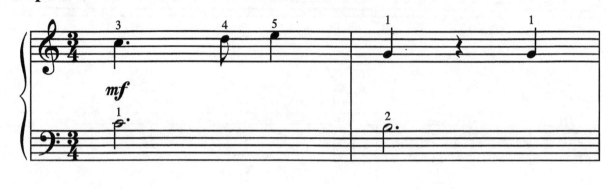

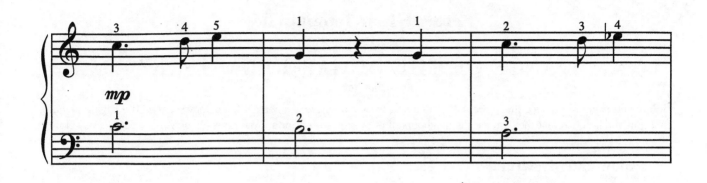

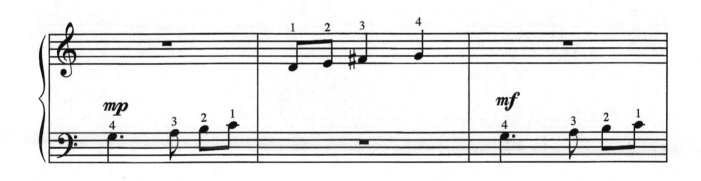

Peter Ilyitch Tchaikovsky

(Russia, 1840–1893)

DANCE OF THE SUGAR PLUM FAIRY

(From *The Nutcracker*)

Before you begin to practice this piece, take a moment to look over the accidentals. They may seem a little frightening at first, but you'll notice that they are usually neighbors of other notes used for a mysterious effect. And of course, pay close attention to the clefs.

Slow and Mysterious

rall.

Alexander Scriabin

(Russia, 1872–1915)

PRELUDE

(Op. 2, No. 1)

Although the Russian Alexander Scriabin went on to compose some of the most exotic, mystical, and revolutionary music in the entire music literature, this piece represents the simplicity he brought to his earliest keyboard pieces. This Prelude is plaintive music, with a kind of barely suppressed emotion just beneath the surface of its flowing melody and rich harmonies.

Andante

Jan Sibelius

(Finland, 1865–1957)

FINLANDIA

(Lyrical theme from the orchestral tone poem, Op. 26)

When Jan Sibelius composed the orchestral tone poem *Finlandia,* he could hardly have imagined the power of its impact on his fellow countrymen. The work came at a time when Finland was under the oppressive domination of Russia and the people hungered for liberation. Filled with explosive outcries from the orchestra's brass and percussion, the music turns to the simple hymn given here: a long passage, growing broader and more emotional—of tender yearning for a simple life in a time of peace.

Moderato

Broad

Johann Strauss, Jr.

(Austria, 1825–1899)

PIZZICATO POLKA

You cannot imagine how popular Johann and his dance orchestra was! His adoring public filled every ballroom he played in, sought tickets to every sold-out concert he gave throughout Europe and Russia, and bought copies of every dance piece he composed. No wonder he was called "King of the Waltz"! "Pizzicato" means "plucked string"—a good guide for playing all those short, light *staccato* notes.

Introduction: *Hesitant and playful*

Playful and light

slightly held back till repeat

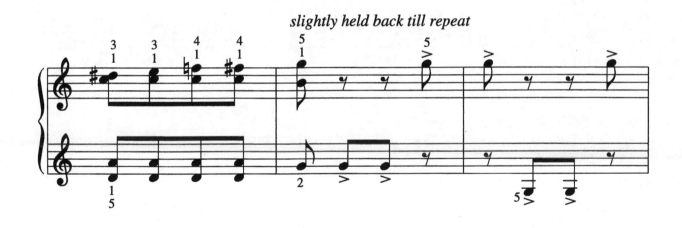

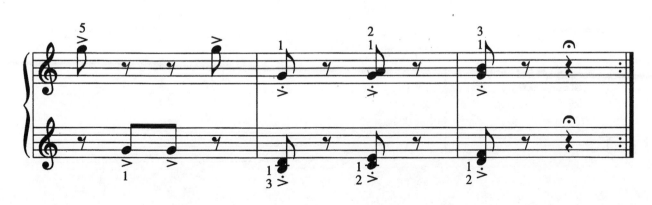

Antonio Vivaldi

(Italy, 1678–1741)

THE AUTUMN HUNT

Almost 300 years ago, in Italy, Antonio Vivaldi composed a collection of "sound-pictures" that magically brought seasonal sights and sounds to the ear. Naming his music *The Four Seasons,* he used violins to imitate bird calls for "Spring," swarms of wasps for "Summer," and icy winds for "Winter." In our piece, he delights us with trotting horses and hunters' horns for "The Autumn Hunt."

Richard Wagner

(Germany, 1813–1883)

BRIDAL PROCESSION

(From the opera *Lohengrin*)

Few of today's brides, bridegrooms and their families realize that the ultra-familiar music that traditionally announces the bride's procession to the altar is actually taken from a nineteenth-century opera about life in Belgium over ten centuries ago! For its most effective performance, it is important not to overdo or exaggerate this theme that everyone knows. Play it in a stately manner, respecting the basic rhythmic idea that fills every measure—in other words, the simpler, the better.

Stately, but not too slow

Richard Wagner

(Germany, 1813–1883)

SONG TO THE EVENING STAR

Tannhäuser is a medieval knight whose feelings are torn between pleasure and prayer, not knowing which way to turn. Wagner composed an opera named after him (pronounced *tahn-hoy-zer*) which is still performed throughout the world. This lovely song to the evening star is sung by Tannhäuser's friend as he waits patiently for the lost, confused knight.

Lento espressivo

Giuseppe Verdi
(Italy, 1813–1901)
GRAND MARCH
(From the opera *Aïda*)

Accompanied by a theater stage chock-full of mounted officers, armed soldiers, bound prisoners—even horses and an elephant or two!—Verdi's Grand March announces the return of Egypt's victorious army from the war front. Here is one of opera's most memorable moments, composed by Giuseppe Verdi for *Aïda*, considered his most popular and important opera. Play it with all of the vigor and pomp appropriate to this magnificent scene.

Maestoso